The Poetry
of My Soul

THE POETRY OF MY SOUL

Love, Honor & Healing

KAREN AULANI HOKE

authorHOUSE®

AuthorHouse™
1663 Liberty Drive
Bloomington, IN 47403
www.authorhouse.com
Phone: 1-800-839-8640

First published by AuthorHouse   02/03/2012

ISBN: 978-1-4685-4985-0 (sc)
ISBN: 978-1-4685-4984-3 (ebk)

Table of Contents

Chapter 3.   Love Hurts47

This book is dedicated to my Dad, Charles Joseph
Hoke, who taught me how to dream . . .

and to my Son, Gabriel Makanani Reyes-Gomez,
who fulfilled the most important one!

With all my love,
Karen (Mom)

CHAPTER 1

FOR DAD

I Miss You, Daddy

I remember when I was a little girl. I used to ask you for a bite of your steak . . . with a playful scolding, I'd open my mouth as you fed me. I miss you, Daddy.

As I got older, you taught me how to be strong. I learned how much you loved to cook and you were so good at planning gatherings. I miss you so much!

I remember how you loved when we'd bake cookies. You loved fresh fruit and popcorn . . . you loved teaching me how to make cheese omelets. The first meal that I cooked by myself was breakfast. Each time I make it now . . . I think of you . . . and I miss you, Daddy.

Most of all, I miss your hugs, your laughter, and your words of wisdom. I try to live by the love you instilled in me and I try to teach my son to do the same. I hope you are looking down on me with pride.

I MISS YOU, DADDY!

It Doesn't Really Matter

It doesn't really matter that

You've been gone for 5 years . . .

It doesn't really matter because

We still wipe away our tears.

It doesn't really matter that

Some say the pain will fade . . .

I doesn't really matter 'cause

We still miss you everyday.

It doesn't really matter that

Some days it's hard to deal . . .

What really matters to us is

"Damn! This hurt is real!"

*Rest in Peace, Pop. We love you . . . *

MAUI BOY

He grew up in Makawao
Mischievous and keen,
Raised by proud Paniolo
Strong and lean.

He loved his life
With those Cowboys on the hill,
Even the ones that taught him
About the till.

Riding through UpCountry
Was always great.
He loved to reminisce
About the ranch in those days.

I remember the stories
He loved to recall.
With a twinkle in his eyes
As he'd inhale the smells.

He'd giggle as he'd tell me
Those tales as a kid,
And laugh continuously
Whenever he did.

Makawao is home . . .
No matter where he lived.
Maui boy forever,
That's just how it is.

We Love You, Pop

With every day that passes, I realize just how much you taught us. Your ability to love was easily instilled in our daily lives from the minute we were all born.

Your laughter was infectious as the chicken pox or the measles.

But, your strength and pride . . . now those traits are the ones that keep us going each day. Keeps us going . . . without you.

We miss you so much that we find ourselves in situations that make us ask ourselves, "what would Dad do???" Now, I myself . . . I can hear your answers sometimes. I can even imagine the look on your face while you are answering me! That's how much you are missed.

So, in reality, it doesn't matter how many years you've been gone. Just the fact that you are not physically with us anymore is devastating enough.

You taught us that life goes on . . . and we realized that your life continues through us. Generation after generation, we will pass on stories of you, and stories that you passed on to us. We will laugh as well as cry when we do so.

It is our way of letting everybody know that you still live on through us.

We love you, Pop!

STAYING STRONG

Some days are really hard . . . challenging, to say the least.

Especially, when evil forces work against me.

Try, as I might, to pray for faith and strength, it is still difficult.

Days of doubts get the best of me on occasion . . . but my heart has prevailed . . . so far.

People always tell me to stay strong and they mean well, but it is easier said than done.

My heart has been crushed and stomped on and shattered so many times throughout my life,

That I feel like a wounded soldier still fighting for love and friendship . . . and survival.

Some days are really hard. Staying strong is really hard . . . but I reach deep within myself to find

The little girl that my father taught to be resilient . . . faithful and true to herself!

Staying strong is hard but it is possible . . . as long as I believe in myself,

Like my father believed in me.

READY

Ready to die
Half way there
Ready to rest
Nobody cares

Trying to please
It's never enough
Can't help crying
Each day is tough

Once in a while
It's ok
Most of the time
I want to go away

Ready to change
My sad life,
Ready to give up
On being a wife

Ready to leave
Ready to die
Ready to join
My Dad in the sky.

MY DADDY

My Daddy is my hero.
Nobody knows the connection I shared with him . . .
Nobody felt the respect and love that we shared . . .
Nobody.

My Daddy loved me for who I was . . .
Just me.

I remember feeling the pull of the Islands
And wondering . . . why?
But when I finally looked him in the eyes,
I knew.
He felt it, too.
Only, he felt it all his life . . .
I was just realizing what "it" was.

He lived every day to teach us how to be
Strong, self reliant, honest
And happy . . . really happy.
He gave us every chance to succeed in life.
And then left it up to us . . .

I pray that I am . . .
Every day that passes.
For him . . . for me . . . and for my son.

My Daddy . . . my Hero!

MAKENA

A special place,
A beautiful beach,
I know when we go there . . .
You're almost within reach.

Makena was your choice,
We scattered you there,
So we visit when we can.
And breathe in the fresh air.

Turtles play in the waves,
As we watch in delight.
Some lift their heads up
As if to say "HI!"

Beautiful Makena,
Is so special to me.
It's where my heart feels closest
To you, Daddy.

CHAPTER 2

SHARING MY HEART

Can't Help But Miss You

Winters here, there's a chill in the air,
And I can't help but miss you.
The decorations are up and the lights are so beautiful,
But I can't help but miss you.

I want to write a letter to Santa,
asking for you as my gift,
But I know that's too much to ask for
because it's GOD you're with.
Yet, I can't help but miss you . . . I just can't help but miss you.

I have my memories to carry me through,
But sometimes those memories, help me miss you!

I wish that a letter to Santa could work,
If only he could make some magic for me . . .
I can't help but miss you.
I just can't stop missing you.

CAN'T GET OVER YOU

Can't seem to forget all that you are,
Won't ever forget that you filled up my heart.
Can't get over you, even though you are gone . . .
Won't stop needing the dream visits till dawn.

Believe in me as I always have, you,
Believe in our friendship, for it is true.
Believe that I need you, even today . . .
Believe that you still help me in every way.

My angel from Heaven, my inspiration, my friend,
You give me the courage that I need deep within.
You know when I need you, as if you were here,
Thank you so much for helping me work passed my fears.

I promise to try to stay strong each day,
I will listen intently for our special song to play.
My heart will beat steady through all it's endeavors,
Your body may be gone but your soul is here forever.

BROKEN

Broken hearts,
Lonely times . . .
Sleepless nights,
Can't unwind.

Pictures hung,
Letters torn . . .
Wishes of never
Being born.

Broken promises,
Stupid lies . . .
Yet still seeing love
In those eyes.

Tear stained pillows,
Crying all night . . .
Yet nothing could ever
Make things right.

Broken memories,
Empty hearts . . .
Two souls lost
When torn apart.

ALMOST CHRISTMAS

It's one week from Christmas and I can't shake this sadness,
I wish you were here . . .
It's the first one without you and I think my hearts breaking . . . again.

I didn't want this time to come and I hate to think that you're gone.
But reality is . . . you built us this gift, our family fit.
And here we are, yes, here we are . . . without you . . . I wish you were
here.

It's one week from Christmas and I can't shake this sadness,
I wish you were here . . .
It's the second one without you and I think my hearts breaking
All over again.

I don't want this season to come when I realize that you are gone,
You gathered this family each year, with love, laughter and care . . .
But now it's so sad without you . . . oh how I miss you each year!
I just wish you were here.

kahll

Enjoy Life

Always worried . . . insecure.
Always wondering if its immature.
Always waiting for someones' hate . . .
Always sad when it's never late.

Ignore the mean.
Ignore their rudeness.
Ignore the unhappy.
Ignore the stupid.

Remember to live.
Remember to smile.
Remember to laugh . . .
      Every minute of every mile!

Throw out the worries,
Don't be insecure!
It's even ok to be immature!

Forget the haters!
They're not so bad . . .
To be that mean is actually sad.

Enjoy every day.
Enjoy every night.
Enjoy all your loved ones.
And enjoy life!

Even Though You're Gone

A heart full of memories,
Of friendships, old and new,
I try to live my life secured–
But I can't stop missing you.

I remember the first words
You said to me, "Baby you so fine"
I remember all the songs you sang,
Happy that you were mine.

When times got bad and you had gone,
I remember our parting words,
I'd said, "I'll love you always Babe,
No matter how much it hurts."

Throughout the years I've never stopped
Loving you with all my heart.
Not even when you were laid to rest
In that beautiful peaceful park.

It's here as if you never left,
Keeping my heart so strong.
My love for you is still the same
Even though you're gone.

FORGIVE ME

Forgive me my friend
I was trying to help,
Trying to keep you
All to myself.

Forgive me my love
I can't let you leave,
My heart will not survive
If you set me free.

Forgive me my Lord,
I beg you in prayers,
To let him still visit
To show me he cares.

Forgive me, forgive me,
I truly believe,
That you coming to visit
Is a gift my faith needs.

Forgive me Oh Lord,
For needing my friend,
It's too devastating to
Let go just yet.

Forgive me my friend,
With your heart and soul,
I'm sorry it's so difficult
To just let you go.

ETERNAL

My life is full of solitude . . .
Broken promises,
Tender lies,
And shattered dreams don't even exist.

Just me,
In my own world . . .
All alone . . .
Missing you.

Some people call it loneliness . . .
Others say it's peace.

All I know is that
You are no longer a part of the living.
And, if I can't hold you, love you,
Then, why should I love at all?

I wish you could come back . . .
But not even death
Could really make my love stop . . .
                    That is Eternal.

Can't Seem To Find My Way

Can't seem to find my way back
To the family fold.
Don't know where to go,
Don't know how it works
These days.

We are not the same,
We never will be again.
Too much has come to light . . .
Too much has been said.

I stepped back to fix my damaged heart
Only to find that no one understood
Why I needed my space.
I felt blame from some
And ridiculed by others.

I just can't seem to heal
Because it hurts too much.

You Knew

You knew how much I loved you
You knew you controlled my heart
You knew the hold you had on me
You knew it from the start.

You knew just how to hold me
You knew just what to say
You knew that I would do anything
Just to make you stay.

You knew you'd break my heart
You knew that it would be soon
You knew that breaking up with me
Was what you had to do.

You knew I never stopped at all
You knew I never would
You knew that I had tried
But didn't think I could.

You knew I'd be crushed
When I heard that you were sick
I wrote to you immediately
You knew my support was quick.

You wrote to me to say
You knew just how I felt
You thanked me for my friendship
You knew my heart would melt.

Your passing left me devastated
But very thankful, too
You knew that I would always
Truly love and miss you.

You Don't Visit

There were so many years that you would walk into my dreams . . .

So many dreams that felt so real . . .

So many nights with you . . .

I miss your visits . . . I miss those dreams . . . I miss you.

You used to visit me while I slept . . .

But . . . you don't visit me anymore.

Rest in Love and Peace, dear friend.

It's been over 20 years since you've passed,

Yet, it still feels like yesterday, when I had to say goodbye.

Sometimes Love Is Forever

Sometimes love does last a lifetime,
Sometimes it survives the biggest of heartbreaks,
It even withstands separations and new lives,
It even lives beyond husbands and wives.

Sometimes love grows passed years of absence,
And even when you think it's over and done,
It sneaks up to surprise you . . .
Because you are definitely "the one" to someone.

Sometimes love is forever,
And it lives beyond the grave.
I knew it would last forever,
The day you went away.

SISTERS

A bond from birth,
A love so strong,
A playmate and a friend.
A sisters voice,
A sisters hug,
Is never just pretend.

In life you grow,
You learn, you love,
You protect each other's hearts.
You give the gift of strength
And guidance,
Even when apart.

Never perfect,
Arguments form,
But time can heal the hurt.
Just never forget
She was your first friend,
Starting from your birth.

SADNESS

Solitude, silence, sadness, survival . . .
Stay hidden, stay quiet, stay safe till tomorrow.
Day by day, night by night,
They don't understand, but that's all right.

Changes in life, changes like death,
Changes that make everyone forget,
I have a hard time to let people go,
When I've loved them so much and it often showed.

No one can understand, not even a bit,
My quest, my journey, had a different fit.
Relationships made, trust was given,
Betrayal behind me as we continued living.

Now solitude is needed, silence is golden,
Sadness is filled with sorrow in every moment.

NAPILI BAY

So perfect, so pretty,
so picturesque and pristine . . .
So much more to my family,
than just another pretty beach.

It's history runs deeper,
than what people read.
It's like the blood in our veins,
this sand and this sea.

Napili Bay tells a story,
with each wave that breaks . . .
there's laughter and tears,
in these memories we make.

It is home, it is heartfelt,
it has a calming affect,
it is so special to our family,
it is where we connect.

The waters have a voice,
for it calls to our souls,
it's the pathway to Heaven,
that our family knows.

It is our doorway to the past,
and our joy of today,
with many fond memories
to still come our way.

KAHLL

My Angel

Even knowing that you were only given months to live

Didn't ease the devastation of knowing that I would never

Be able to hug you again.

I was not able to attend your funeral but had I gone,

I would have died myself seeing you lying in your coffin.

I go to your grave as often as possible but I find comfort

In the thought that because I didn't see them bury you,

You might still be out there . . . alive and well.

In my heart, I know you're gone.

Yet, in my soul, you are ever present.

As sure as I breathe today,

You are an important part of my life.

You are my friend, my superstar, my Angel.

I miss you!

MAYBE

Today I woke up with the feeling that you were here,

Walking, talking, laughing and singing . . . with me.

It was exciting but yet bittersweet.

It made me want to go right back to sleep and dream about you again.

It felt so real.

Sometimes I think that it's GOD telling me that I found love once, so it's not impossible.

For whatever its meaning . . . I miss you so much. I have not stopped loving you . . . and I never will.

Someday I will see you again. Maybe in another life . . . maybe.

Lyrics

All things tell a story.
All words come alive.
Some make you happy.
While others make you cry.

Those with a melody,
Grab your heart strings.
Some with a rhythm . . .
Gives you dancing feet.

Words to the music.
Beats and sounds.
Swaying with your partner,
Going 'round and 'round.

Jumpin' n jivin'
Or slow dancing so sweet.
it continues the story
Of your words to a beat.

LITTLE GIRL LOVE

When I was a little girl, I fell in love with you. Even though you broke my heart, I wouldn't give up on you.

I remember the party that we went to and I asked you to slow dance. You held me in your arms and my world began its trance. That night confirmed my feelings . . . the commitment of my heart.

I loved you as a little girl . . . and then, I just never stopped.

That little girl grew up with that unconditional love. It's what gave me the strength to go on after the illness made you succumb.

Now, all I have is our dance to remind me of the comfort of your embrace . . . until I see you once again when I enter Heavens Gates.

LAHAINA

High above this town you see,
 it's history beyond the trees.
Majestic and wondrous, beckoning those
 adventurous visitors souls.

At waters edge you see an "L"
 engraved upon the mountainside.
Sometimes natural,
 and sometimes white . . .
 to many it's so easy to find.

It's stands for the town,
 small and inviting . . .
with stories of tradition
 in the education it's providing.

Imua Lahainaluna!
Can be heard in the winds.
 as our ancestors chantings
 echo within.

Celebrations are many,
 for all walks of life . . .
But the people come together
 on one special night.

They yell, "Light it up!"
 and wait to see,
 their beautiful "L" shining
 as bright as can be.

On that one day each year,
 it sends a message to the town . . .
 that Commencement is over,
  as the graduates stand proud.

Rich with history,
 Unfailing with pride,
 Lahaina is the heartbeat of the West Side!

LAUGHTER AND TEARS

I started my day with a smile . . .
I dreamt about him.
When my alarm woke me up,
His smile started to fade but he told me
Through his laughter "don't worry, I will visit you again."

I jumped out of bed, happy for the lift,
I prayed to the LORD my thanks for HIS gift.
I know that it hurts because he died so young . . .
But I laughed as I cried because he's not really gone.

I only wish that his family could experience the joy
That he gives to me, when my world is in need . . .
but I still long to hear his laughter all day.
His voice will never really go away.

LAHAINA SUNSET

I love to see the sunsets
From Lahaina Town.
They are the best to see
All year round.

All so very beautiful . . .
Yet unique as each his own,
The colors blending perfectly . . .
Vibrant in their tones.

I love to watch the sun descend
As if to hide in the sea.
Love to see the horizon
As pretty as can be.

Nowhere else in this world is more beautiful,
Than sunsets next the Lanai.
Unless, of course, it's the ones
On the shores off Molokai!

I Remember The Day

I remember the day that I was told about your diagnosis . . . the tears wouldn't stop, and the question 'why' echoed in my mind and heart.

I knew then, that I needed to contact you . . . I needed to call you, to hear your beautiful voice.

I wrote to you, you wrote back . . . and I read your letter through tears of pride and also, sadness.

I always knew that you were brave, and strong, and handsome . . .

But with this situation everyone else realized it too . . .

Those wonderful qualities are my inspiration each day, to never give up . . . and you never did.

Even through the pain and sickness, the pills and the Doctors, you never gave up.

Heart and soul strong, you gave life the best that you had in the short time that you graced us with your presence.

I remember the day of your passing . . . a part of me died with you,

But a part of you will live on in me for the rest of my life.

I Love This Man

Today I know that
I love this man.
For all of my life,
He'll be my friend.
For whatever it's worth,
He inspires my faith.
Whenever I need him,
I don't hesitate.

Today, I look back,
So many years have passed,
But I know that he loves me,
My friend from the past.
I know that we share
A bond that endures,
I know that we share
A heart that is pure.

Today I know that
I love this man,
I've loved him since
We first became friends.
For the rest of my life
And even beyond,
We will share one heart,
For our love is strong.

Haleakala

Perfect sunrise,
Perfect scene,
Vibrantly golden,
With orange sunbeams.

Fluffy clouds,
Pillowy white,
Mysterious wonder,
As sun awakens sky.

Chill in the air,
Awaiting dawn,
Warmth enveloping,
In its rising sun.

FOCUS

Focus on the Lord
And all that HIS love provides . . .
Stay faithful, stay strong,
Feel the warmth of HIS light.

Do not worry or stress,
Place it all in HIS hands . . .
Give it all to our Lord,
Instead of relying on man.

Put your hands palm to palm,
Point your fingers to the sky,
Close your eyes and pray
For all your loved ones tonight.

Ask the Lord for unity,
Ask HIM for understanding,
Ask HIM for humility
And patience for the demanding.

Keep your sights on HIS words,
Keep your heart on HIS sleeve,
Keep your focus on redemption,
And HE will help you in times of need.

RUN AWAY

I think of going home sometimes
But I've made a home here as well.
Funny thing though . . .
I don't feel like I belong in either place.

If home is where the heart is,
And my heart is broken,
Where do I go?
What do I do?

If I could run away,
I'd do it now.

SOMETIMES

Sometimes life throws us curveballs that are so effective
that they psych us out on the first pitch.
Sometimes things happen because they need to,
even if you don't really want them to.
Sometimes we believe that we are too old to deal with
the heartaches and the headaches that life sends our way.
But, we are never too old to love or hate,
be happy or sad,
or feel crowded or lonely.

Sometimes it takes us longer than others
to find that special person to share our life with.
And, sometimes,
people share their lives with those that are not worthy
because they settle for not being lonely.

When it's time to love,
love with all your heart
because you may not ever get the chance to again.

Every Day That You're Not Here

Every time I think about you,
Every time I heard your voice,
My heart would race like a shooting star . . .
    across the sky.

No one could ever know,
    the pain I feel, the sadness grows . . .
Even though it's been years,
my heart still breaks every day . . .
    that you're not here.

I cried the day we lost you,
I cried each day since you've been gone.
Nobody knows,
    the pain in me, the sadness grows.
Even though it's been years . . .
      my heart still breaks every day
        that you're not here.

Somewhere In Heaven

Somewhere in Heaven,
This I know,
Perched on a cloud,
Hoping we are alright . . .
We have our moments,
We cry our tears,
We wipe them away
And resume our routine.
We knew this was coming,
We were not sure when . . .
It was just more devastating
Losing both of you within weeks.
We have our memories,
We share our pain . . .
We all love you both
And that is a given.
I know that you are
In good company now.
Reunited with both your parents
And the rest of our loved ones.
One day we hope
To join you both,
One day we pray
To be perched on our own cloud,
Hoping those living are alright.
Your bodies were old,
Your spirits stayed strong,
I thank God for the time with you both,
And can wait to see you again!

Uncle Bruce

As I watched them cry for their devastating loss,
I think of him greeting his Lord and his Spouse . . .

His Mother, his Father, Sisters and Brothers . . .
All of his loved ones . . . even Grandfathers and Grandmothers.

I cry as well, with mixed emotions of grieving,
For I know that salvation was what he was needing.

A release of his spirit from the body that aged,
To soar with the Angels that guide his way.

The pain is gone, bedridden no more,
Infections all healed, Thank You Lord!

Sail through the Heavens, don't worry about us,
We will help each other cope with our physical loss.

Dear Aunty Ulu,

I would like to tell you just what you mean to me . . .

You are not only my Mothers' Sister, you are my special Aunty. My mother figure while my mother was not present. You let me move into your home and taught me what love and responsibility and independence really is. You guided me through my adult years and helped me to become the person that I am today. You helped me raise my son and saw me through the heartache of divorce. You accepted my life without so much as a slap in the head . . . and for that, I love you! Your love, financial support and guidance helped to save my husband from being sent away from me. We celebrate 15 years together and we are so thankful to you for that gift.

I think I understood you because you understood me. We were not always respected or looked upon with intelligence but we dealt with it and carried on. Our hearts share the same devotion to our family and the Aina. We just couldn't make miracles happen the way that we wanted to.

You know that I love you . . . and I will not ever stop!

Mahalo, Aunty Ulu . . . you may not physically be here with us any longer but you will forever be in my heart. As God taught us to love for eternity, I am sure he intended that to be because of special people like you.

Love,

Karen

More Time To Heal

How can I love people so much but yet not want to see them or be an active part of their lives?

Some want to know why . . . but out of loyalties and commitments, only half truths are given.

As I get older, and loved ones pass on, I find myself hiding more. The comforts of my home are what keeps me sane. Sometimes the lost is just too much . . . just too painful . . . just too overwhelming.

I used to feel so lost and alone.

Now, years later, solitude is my friend . . . my savior.

It doesn't mean that I love them all less,

It just means that I need more time to heal.

Chapter 3

Love Hurts

Before It's Too Late

You are supposed to be my partner, my best friend, my protector . . .
Yet here I am, trying to get through each day without crying.
You make me feel disrespected and unloved, unworthy and taken advantage of.
Sometimes . . . you even make me feel like I don't want to go on.

That is when I need my space . . . my alone time . . . my crying therapy . . . my time to
Ask the LORD for understanding and strength.

I feel as if I am losing you . . . well, the 'you' that I love so much.
I know that I have so much more living to do.
I know that I have a lot of dreams and goals to reach.
But . . . you still manage to bring me to the ground and stomp all over my heart.

I will say today, that I will reach down into my heart and find the will to survive . . .
The faith to believe in myself and the hope that the 'you' that I love will find his
Way back to me before it's too late.
kahll

If You Ever

If you ever loved me the way that I needed you to,
You'd be here . . .
Ready, willing and able,
To make my pain go away . . .
To dry my tears . . .
And to hold me in the comfort of your arms every moment that you
could.

If you ever really loved me the way that I needed you to,
You never would have shut me out all those years ago.
You would have held me in your arms,
And told me that you would never let me go!
But, you were young and headstrong . . .
And your ego was damaged.

If you ever loved me the way that I needed you to,
You would have fought harder to save our relationship . . . instead of
letting it go so easily.

If you ever really loved me . . .
You never would have broke my heart again,
After you knew that it was so hard for me to piece it back together when
I moved away.

I can see it now,
Even though it hurts . . .
That you never really loved me at all.

HAPPY BIRTHDAY TO ME

I look at your picture with tears in my eyes,
Trying to make sense out of all the lies,
So much denial, so much restraint,
Wishing you'd acknowledge the love we've maintained.

Today is my birthday,
All I want is you,
But it's not going to happen,
no matter what I do.

I'll smile and pretend
that everything's alright,
Like all my past birthdays,
I won't see you tonight.

I'll carry on today,
Just like the day before,
Hoping and praying that
You'll walk through the door.

Being older today,
Makes me kind of sad,
Over half of my life missing you
Really makes me mad.

But, despite the anger,
And aside from the pain,
All I really want
is to hold you again.

Happy Birthday to me!

I STILL WISH

Ready to go, ready to move on.
Ready to not be with you, I'm just about done.

Too much arguing, too much hate,
Too much power trips, this is my fate.

Sad and depressed, frustrated and misunderstood.
I have even doubted leaving the hood.

Going full circle, still needing your strength.
Will you inspire me to reach out to my faith?

So very lonely without your whispers of guidance,
I want to just give in so I don't have to fight this.

Ready to meet HIM face to face.
But not ready to leave my child in disgrace.

Continuing on . . . regardless of the pain.
Yet I still wish to sit and talk with you again.

I STAND ALONE

I guess I should not be surprised. The vacation was too much fun. Too nice. Too happy. I had a flash of doubt . . . a wandering thought. What if? A knot in my stomach, just beginning. Is he like THEM? Does he have so little love for me that he could betray me and our marriage? I did not listen to my thoughts. I pushed away my doubt. Yet here we are today, a knife in my back and a feeling of loneliness that makes me suicidal.

I am alone. Now and forever . . . alone. No one can save me. No one can see the pattern of the last 15 years, quite like me. His lies define him. His denials come full circle.

I stand alone. I stand alone.

I Can't Promise You

I can't promise you a lifetime
Of walks along the beach.
I can't promise you eternities
Of rubbing your tired feet.

I can't give you all the hugs I can
Because you couldn't stay
But I realize our destinies
Have made me live this way.

All I have left are memories,
Through pictures and songs.
All my poems tell of the heartaches
Of where my life went wrong.

I can't promise you the world
But I sure do wish I could.
I wanted to give you my soul,
For inspirations good.

I can't promise you the moon
Or a kiss upon your cheek.
But I can promise you forever . . .
My love for you,
Eternally.

FREE MY HEART

You've played with my heart long enough.

I refuse to let you hurt me anymore.

I have promised you the world and I have nothing but tears to show for all my love and devotion.

You've stomped on my heart and left me sad too many times. I have finally come to my senses.

I am ready to free my heart of you.

Exuded

I lay down my head to rest,
A sadness settles above my chest.
Dispare and defeat ever so near,
Why do I have to continue in tears?

I dread the tomorrows
That are like today.
I hate the grumpy mean man
In my way.

Is happiness too much
To ask for right now?
Not even for Christmas, apparently.
Wow!

If only I could run,
Hide somewhere secluded,
From the heartache in the world,
That my life has exuded.
kah

ANGRY

Frustration, fear,

Uncertain . . . for years.

Uneasy, alone,

Longing for home.

Desperate, afraid,

Temptations rage.

Unhappy, upset,

Full of regret.

Hurt, untrue,

Angry at you.

All I Really Want

Trying to heal,
Hoping to mend,
Bad situations,
Missing a friend.

Closer at heart,
Yet shouldn't be,
coping with fate,
and our destiny.

Making no difference,
Mind over heart . . .
Problems that made
Our life fall apart.

Moments of honesty,
Then the wall builds again . . .
When will I ever have
To cease to pretend?

Presently continuing,
Moving on as I'm told to . . .
But all I really want
Is just to hold you.

JUSTIFY

Justify the heartache,
Wipe away the tears,
Realize the healing
Beyond all of your fears.

You know he'll never change,
You know his hearts not yours,
You know he will continue to hurt you,
If you don't close that door.

Justify your self worth,
Cleanse away the pain,
Realize you are stronger
Than when you first began.

Utilize your strengths,
Carry on with life.
Remember how you hurt.
Relinquish him from your life.

No Choice

I yearn for romance,
For a protector,
For love.
I want special kisses,
Slow dances . . .
Warm hugs.

I wish for someone
To love me for "me",
I hope for a man
To make my heart complete.
I yearn for romantic
Walks on the beach,
I want to feel love
Making my heart beat.

Some nights I dream
Of candlelit meetings,
Beautiful music
And spontaneous greetings.

Flowers and cards,
Sweet words of affection.
A sign of my love
Seen in reflections.

I yearn for romance,
But reality today . . .
I settled for a companion
To get through the days.

No One

No one is going to understand
    What you've meant to me . . .
No one knows the pain I've suffered
    Or my sacrifices for thee.

No one can ever tell me,
    That all in love is fair . . .
No one will ever see
    The heartache behind my tears.

No one reaches out to comfort
    The person deep in me . . .
No one to promise a life of joy
    Or a love to set me free.

Not Long Ago

Not long ago you told me a special secret . . .

You told me to believe in our love and nothing or no one could ever break us apart.

Nobody could have believed in you and our love, more than I . . .

But, yet, today I live a very separate life . . . far away from you.

How could you tell me the secret, yet not believe yourself?

Not long ago . . . I thought you believed in me . . . and in us.

ONE WORLD

Take my breath away from me,
hold it close then set it free,
the kiss would mean so much . . .

Wrap me in your arms again,
Hold me close, don't pretend,
That we are just friends now . . .

Hand in hand, face to face,
Smiling, laughing, enjoying our space,
Our worlds are one.

Tell Me Please

Are we just wasting time?
Should we just move on with our lives today?

I know I love you boy but I'm not sure where you stand with me.
For once, tell me, please.
Tell me, please.

One day you're full of hugs, kisses and smiles so bright-
The next, you are so unhappy—nothing I do is right.

I know I love you boy but I'm not sure where I stand with you.
For once, tell me, please.
Please tell me, oh please.

What Good Is Pride

Sometimes I think about you so much
that I can feel you near me.
I know that you are far away
But when the love is still strong . . .
no matter where you go,
              it will find you.

Sometimes I imagine you
knocking at my door.
Maybe one day you will.
But stubborn pride can be strong too.

What good is pride,
If you can't find our love, again?

Puppy Love

A school girl crush,
called Puppy Love.
Carried through a lifetime,
Then, to Heaven above.
Some don't remember,
How could I ever forget?
What you've meant to my life,
Dear memories I protect.
I carry on daily,
Although it's a chore,
I draw on your strengths,
If the tears start to pour.
I've turned to your spirit,
I've called on my faith,
To get me through,
The hardest of days.
After all these years,
I do believe,
That our paths
Were meant to meet.
Puppy Love,
Innocent and sweet,
Is now Eternally
Imbedded in me.

Never Guaranteed

Love is never guaranteed,
it is a gift, a blessing.
True love is given straight from the heart,
No stipulations or restrictions or negotiations.
Often times it is an abused gift.
But when it is pure and honest,
It can make the world a better place.